HAL•LEONARD®
VIOLIN PLAY-ALONG

AUDIO ACCESS INCLUDED

LINDSEY STIRLING
TOP SONGS

PLAYBACK+
Speed • Pitch • Balance • Loop

To access audio visit:
www.halleonard.com/mylibrary

Enter Code
4100-6168-4133-7734

Photo courtesy of Devin Graham

ISBN 978-1-5400-3651-3

Jon Vriesacker, violin
Audio arrangements by Peter Deneff
Recorded and Produced by Jake Johnson
at Paradyme Productions

For all works contained herein:
Unauthorized copying, arranging, adapting, recording, Internet posting, public performance,
or other distribution of the music in this publication is an infringement of copyright.
Infringers are liable under the law.

Visit Hal Leonard Online at
www.halleonard.com

Contact us:
Hal Leonard
7777 West Bluemound Road
Milwaukee, WI 53213
Email: info@halleonard.com

In Europe, contact:
Hal Leonard Europe Limited
42 Wigmore Street
Marylebone, London, W1U 2RN
Email: info@halleonardeurope.com

In Australia, contact:
Hal Leonard Australia Pty. Ltd.
4 Lentara Court
Cheltenham, Victoria, 3192 Australia
Email: info@halleonard.com.au

Beauty and the Beast Medley

from Walt Disney's BEAUTY AND THE BEAST
Music by ALAN MENKEN
Lyrics by HOWARD ASHMAN
Arranged by Lindsey Stirling

© 1991 Wonderland Music Company, Inc. and Walt Disney Music Company
This arrangement © 2017 Wonderland Music Company, Inc. and Walt Disney Music Company
All Rights Reserved. Used by Permission.

SOMETHING THERE

GASTON

Fast Waltz

allarg.

allarg. molto

BE OUR GUEST
Fast

BELLE
Soaring

BEAUTY AND THE BEAST
Tranquil

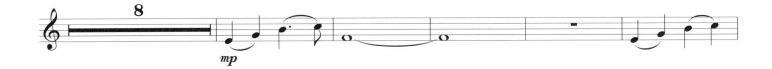

Energetic

Slower

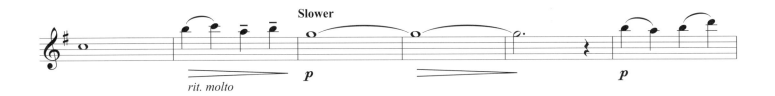

Boulevard of Broken Dreams

Words by Billie Joe
Music by Green Day
Arranged by Lindsey Stirling

© 2004 WB MUSIC CORP. and GREEN DAZE MUSIC
All Rights Administered by WB MUSIC CORP.
All Rights Reserved   Used by Permission

Dragonborn
(Skyrim Theme)

By Jeremy Soule
Arranged by Lindsey Stirling and Peter Hollens

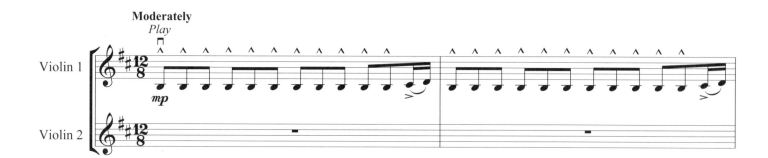

© 2011 Zenimax Music Publishing
All Rights Administered by PEN Music Group, Inc.
All Rights Reserved   Used by Permission

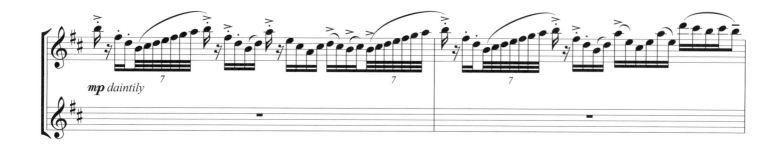

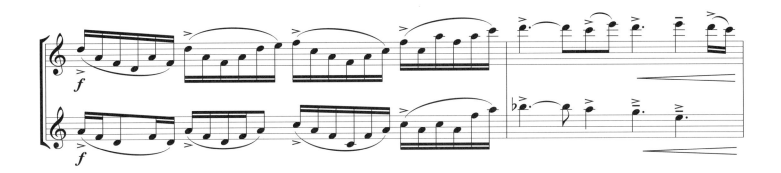

The Greatest Showman Medley

Words and Music by Benj Pasek and Justin Paul
Arranged by Lindsey Stirling

Moderately
A MILLION DREAMS

NEVER ENOUGH

Copyright © 2017 Breathelike Music, Pick In A Pinch Music and T C F Music Publishing, Inc.
This arrangement Copyright © 2018 Breathelike Music, Pick In A Pinch Music and T C F Music Publishing, Inc.
All Rights for Breathelike Music and Pick In A Pinch Music Administered Worldwide by Kobalt Songs Music Publishing
All Rights Reserved   Used by Permission

REWRITE THE STARS

It Ain't Me

Words and Music by Ali Tamposi, Selena Gomez,
Andrew Wotman, Kyrre Gorvell-Dahll and Brian Lee
Arranged by Lindsey Stirling

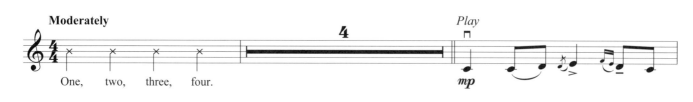

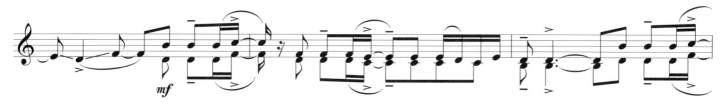

Copyright © 2017 Reservoir 416, Universal Music Corp., SMG Tunes, Andrew Watt Music,
Sony/ATV Music Publishing Allegro (UK), Warner-Tamerlane Publishing Corp. and Songs From The Dong
All Rights for SMG Tunes Administered by Universal Music Corp.
All Rights for Andrew Watt Music Administered by Songs Of Kobalt Music Publishing
All Rights for Sony/ATV Music Publishing Allegro (UK) Administered by
Sony/ATV Music Publishing LLC, 424 Church Street, Suite 1200, Nashville, TN 37219
All Rights for Songs From The Dong Administered by Warner-Tamerlane Publishing Corp.
All Rights Reserved   Used by Permission

Senbonzakura

Words and Music by Drum Tao
Arranged by Lindsey Stirling

Copyright © 2017 UNIVERSAL MUSIC PUBLISHING LLC and UNIVERSAL - POLYGRAM INTERNATIONAL TUNES, INC.
All Rights Reserved   Used by Permission

Stampede

Words and Music by Mark Ballas, Lindsey Stirling and Brittany Jean Carlson

Copyright © 2018 BMG Platinum Songs, Can't Spell Ballas Without Balls Music, Songs Of Stone Buddah,
Lindseystomp Music, LLC, Songs Of Universal, Inc. and BC Jean Publishing
All Rights for BMG Platinum Songs, Can't Spell Ballas Without Balls Music and Songs Of Stone Buddah Administered by
BMG Rights Management (US) LLC
All Rights for BC Jean Publishing Administered by Songs Of Universal, Inc.
All Rights Reserved   Used by Permission

CODA

* optional part in cue notes

Hi-Lo

Words and Music by Amy Lee and William Barry Hunt
Arranged by Lindsey Stirling

Copyright © 2017 BMG Firefly, Spaceway Music and Professor Screweye Publishing
All Rights Administered by BMG Rights Management (US) LLC
All Rights Reserved   Used by Permission

High _____ or low. _

You're nev - er far ___ be - neath _ me and I _____

gave up on _ you. _ But I nev - er

for - got.